Things and Flesh

Things and Flesh

POEMS BY

Linda Gregg

To Jim
Best Wishes
Linda Gregg

2002

Graywolf Press
Saint Paul, Minnesota

Publication of this volume is made possible in part by a grant provided
by the Minnesota State Arts Board through an appropriation by the
Minnesota State Legislature, and by a grant from the National
Endowment for the Arts. Significant support has also been provided
by Dayton's, Mervyn's, and Target stores through the Dayton Hudson
Foundation, the Bush Foundation, the McKnight Foundation, the
General Mills Foundation, the St. Paul Companies, and other generous
contributions from foundations, corporations, and individuals. To these
organizations and individuals we offer our heartfelt thanks.

Published by Graywolf Press
2402 University Avenue, Suite 203
Saint Paul, Minnesota 55114
All rights reserved.

www.graywolfpress.org

Published in the United States of America

ISBN 1-55597-293-4

2 4 6 8 9 7 5 3 1
First Graywolf Printing, 1999

Library of Congress Catalog Card Number: 99-60734

Cover design: Julie Metz
Cover photograph: Linda Gregg

Contents

∙‿ Things and Flesh

The book should be heavy with things and flesh.

ALBERT CAMUS

The Precision

There is a modesty in nature. In the small
of it and in the strongest. The leaf moves
just the amount the breeze indicates
and nothing more. In the power of lust, too,
there can be a quiet and clarity, a fusion
of exact moments. There is a silence of it
inside the thundering. And when the body swoons,
it is because the heart knows its truth.
There is directness and equipoise in the fervor,
just as the greatest turmoil has precision.
Like the discretion a tornado has when it tears
down building after building, house by house.
It is enough, Kafka said, that the arrow fit
exactly into the wound that it makes. I think
about my body in love as I look down on these
lavish apple trees and the workers moving
with skill from one to the next, singing.

Variously Us

Something breaches the ocean of doctrine,
heaving sideways amid the splattering
and squall. Our assumptions harpooned
into the storm of being. The heft and slop
of consciousness beginning inside
what we call our life. And below,
under the roaring dark, is the silver sheen
and scale of silence. The spirit apart.
The whale of us gathering color to itself
all the gradations between black and white
according to what depth and the degree
of transparence. Rising and falling back.
Faith translated into muscle and invisible bone.
We and it joined like the scene painted over
and over on the ancient Athenian vases
of a man struggling with a fierce-jawed lion.
The ship of us battened down in the storm
of mystery. Always refracted. We are lashed
to our body. Swamped in the loving,
the pods of prayer, the seeds of finally.
Hot blood breathing far down, the harpoon
of the mind wedged in us, shaping.

Alone with the Goddess

The young men ride their horses fast
on the wet sand of Pangaritis.
Back and forth, with the water sliding
up to them and away.
This is the sea where the goddess lives,
angry, her lover taken away.
Don't wear red, don't wear green here,
the people say. Do not swim in the sea.
Give her an offering.
I give a coconut to protect
the man I love. The water pushes it back.
I wade out and throw it farther.
"The goddess does not accept your gift,"
an old woman says.
I say perhaps she likes me
and we are playing a game.
The old woman is silent,
the horses wear blinders of cloth,
the young men exalt in their bodies,
not seeing right or left, pretending
to be brave. Sliding on and off
their beautiful horses
on the wet beach at Pangaritis.

The Calves Not Chosen

The mind goes *caw, caw, caw, caw,*
dark and fast. The orphan heart
cries out, "Save me. Purchase me
as the sun makes the fruit ripe.
I am one with them and cannot feed
on winter dawns." The black birds
are wrangling in the fields
and have no kindness, all sinew
and stick bones. Both male and female.
Their eyes are careless of cold and rain,
of both day and night. They love nothing
and are murderous with each other.
All things of the world are bowing
or being taken away. Only a few calves
will be chosen, the rest sold for meat.
The sound of the wind grows bigger
than the tree it's in, lessens only
to increase. *Haw, haw* the crows call,
awake or asleep, in white, in black.

Calamities: Another Eden

Out beyond what we imagine.
Out beyond the familiar, leaving home
and being homeless. Breaching the seas,
foundering on a coast in the West,
searching along coastlines in the Far East.
The heart is left and leaves,
stands in each part of the farness
away from the other. Living in each
particular moment of the day,
of present claims and the careless claims
of always. The ocean pushes out,
pushes the heart into the unknown,
toward the middle of a self that yearns
and remembers. The spirit is rejected
and walks slowly out of another Eden.
An Eden that is not the heart,
is homelessness, is isolate. The heart
is gathered into the familiar nothingness
and held. Is held and sent forth.
In the way a seal drops into the water,
sliding like oil in its element.
Turns and rolls. What we call happiness.
The seasons change and change,
west and east, tropical and far
northern. What we call love.
Heaven is deep and deeper. We leave
and leave into the questing.

The Center of Intent

Is there a lesson in the way this new silence lasts?
Is it like the river's genius for making the water
the same shape constantly as it pours between
these two boulders? Is there some reason
why the bird is always hungry and the body
never gone? What explains the odor
of the sea grass here? Why must we bow down,
yield to the flowering? Maybe love is the Lord's trap.
Maybe He sees us as the tree leaning over the stream.
Perhaps He can't experience the difference between
our pain, our loneliness, and the heron flying
through the special silence at evening.

Not a Pretty Bird

She was not a nightingale
as the Greek said.
Philomela was a woman.
The sister of the new wife.
Raped, tongue cut out by the husband.
Locked away.
Not a swallow, not the bird of morning
and late evenings that end so swiftly.
Not a myth. She was a girl.
That is the story: the empty mouth,
the bloody breasts. The outrage.
Not the transformation.

She Writes to the Man Who Writes of Her in His Poems

You tried to hide me in darkness,
tried to live half of your time with me
in the dark. You invented me.
Finally went back to your people.
Were obedient. Were received
with praise. But in the supermarket
you suddenly needed to know
where I was. Turned to face
each direction of the universe
there in the aisle. But nowhere
did anything return to you.
I am here in this morning
with your picture on the table,
leaning against a vase of flowers.
(One of them has fallen in my sleep.)
A bird is singing, repeating
itself over and over. And over.

The Spirit Neither Sorts nor Separates

There is a flower. We call it God.
It closes and opens and dies.
We still call it God. There is a stone
that does nothing and is still God.
Everything is of Heaven. There is mud
around the edge of the pond.
There are reeds, water lilies
and a few dragonflies. The pond is light
and dark and warm because of the sun.
Hidden fish. The air itself.
The bush outside is full of three and four
kinds of birds. Winter birds instead
of leaves. The snow over ground is enough.
The birds hopping and feeding
and departing are flowers,
a mouth singing, your heart the way it was.

As Being Is Eternal

She is sitting alone in the bright room.
There are two other rooms, one dark
and closed, the other with a single light.
Outside there is a cold November.
She is remembering the statues
she saw in Greece on the mountain,
in empty rooms where light was added
to light, surrounded by silence.
They seemed ready to be seen.
The way one hears a door quietly
close and footsteps coming closer.
Present and past like that. The way
art is exact. Like the woman
in her lighted room.
She could rise and walk
into one of the empty rooms
that she is not in. Could see
a vase of red roses on the table
where white roses were last week.
Time has finished its journey,
has come its long half way.
The air is heavy as water as she
bends her head over the page.

Gypsy Kings

Another late afternoon and I am sitting in
a half-lotus on my exercise mat watching
two pigeons walking around the broken bricks
as I listen to the empty passion of the Gypsy Kings
on my Walkman. I see the birds from underneath
as they fly up, just before they change from flying
to landing on the overhead above me. Pink feet
and red eyes, necks that shine like grease
on wet streets. You might say
this is a leftover life I am living.
I know some Ezra Pound by heart. I know Wallace
Stevens almost more than I want to.
Two women came today to judge me
for an almost boyfriend's mother.
But I moved first. I was in a very good mood
because Ai had made me another unknown soup,
so I told them how lovely their jewelry was
and won them over. They put thumbs up,
told me I was beautiful.
Mentioned Lolo and wrote down
their addresses for me.
One mentioned her own son.

The Heart Flowing Out

All things we see are the shapes death makes.
When we see straightly and hard we see
with the eyes of death. Light and dark, the weight
of the forms: a bell, a door, in their placement
one with the other. The black window
and the white wall are taut in their exact
distance, and firm in themselves,
surrounded by the imperfect dark hills
and the absolute light of the sky. Feeling is not
in the things, but in us. Though sometimes
they shake like a vision in their perfect tension
of being. Death is strong, so the world is
that strong too. A man walks down a road
then cuts across a field. We walk
with our soft bodies and tough minds.
Water is the shine moving, death does not flow.
We flow, our bodies and hearts flow.
When we enter death it gives way,
but not yet. Our hearts flow out through
the consciousness, focused.
The more it looks, the more it sees the hard
thing shaking with its own energy
in relation to the whole scene and its meaning.
Making that meaning, whatever it means.

The Empty Bowl

You know when to wake me in the dark
of the soul, your people singing a drone
without doctrine: *a lamb, a lamb, a lamb,
a lamb.* You know when to open our hands
and let what we are holding fall down.
Show us as you did in the ripe fields after.
The children crying in the garden,
lamb, lamb. Without residue, without humility.
Your voice, voices. Your voices'
voice. You know when to make the rain,
when to ask for our preparing. We stand
in line with the others, moving forward
without song, without understanding the words.
Love like a bowl, a trial to teach us
how to survive the sweeping, the breaking,
holding in the hands what is cherished
even in its uselessness, even as the bowl
of the mind disappears in the distance,
in the unvisited house where there is
no honey, no bees, the comb dead.
There is only the beginning of each day
with the roosters calling and our voice.
No salt, no bread. Only the chanting:
lamb, lamb, lamb.

More than New

One of the men begins to sing. The woman
turns from side to side, flouncing her skirt
and stomping. The men play their guitars.
He begins to sing again. She stamps harder
but it is not big enough. The man sings
so hard it breaks the song and becomes wailing.
The woman is proud. The men are proud.
Everybody is proud. And it is still not
strong enough. The gods are relaxed, pleased,
but justice is unmoved. Says, "Show me something.
Don't mess with me. Show me something I can believe."

She Had Expected Something Else

Love aroused her like a heifer
in the presence of a bull.
She had expected something else.
She thought the invisible might
show itself as night, or the taste
of air off the sea. She felt it
wading through wildflowers
on a hillside, in the whinnying
of horses and the smell
of their sweat on her jeans.
It was love as the engine
that kept her awake,
something striding across waves
in the dark. Something sending her
from Batu to Prambanan.

Fathers

It was evening when my love and I
got to New York, and winter.
And the apartment was not lovely.
So I said, let's go to the Brooklyn Bridge
and walk across. He said it was cold.
I said it was okay. We'll bundle up
and invent poems for our fathers.
So there we were on the huge bridge.
Beautiful because you are looking at it.
Or because you are walking toward.
Or away. Birds flying through the wires.
Hart Crane's seagulls. Whitman,
America, my father. And me. My love
was walking, but not happily.
Shamed in the disorder of not knowing.
This is big, I say. This is the most visionary
place in the United States. But it does not
help, because he's Chinese. Bulk and grace,
I say. Weight and refinement.
Vision both common and religious.
Our fathers, dead in America,
the spirits singing.

Etiology

Cruelty made me. Cruelty and the sweet smelling earth,
and the wet scent of bay. The heave in the rumps
of horses galloping. Heaven forbid that my body not
perish with the rest. I have smelled the rotten wood
after rain and watched maggots writhe on
dead animals. I have lifted the dead owl while it
was still warm. Heaven forbid that I should be saved.

So Different from Heaven

On a day with heavy rain I went with two men
into a room filled with a whole orchestra
of dusty gamelan. The two of them played a long time
in the dull light. Until an old custodian came in
and, without saying anything, joined the other two.
Later, he stood silent on the porch facing the wet
courtyard with that look adult men here have
of already knowing about death. Eternity made
of fervor, so different from Heaven.
The sun is hot. The moon lessens and regains.
I am sure it is the only life that God can taste.

The Soul Ripening

The sun is so bright and the air so clear
that a thing seen in this light is bigger
than it is. The two cows in a field
are magnified just as the brown of the one
under the olive tree is made richer
by the shade. And the sea now is made
a different blue by time as I walk
back up the path this evening.

Fish Tea Rice

It is on the Earth that all things transpire,
and only on the Earth. On it, up out of it,
down into it. Wading and stepping, pulling
and lifting. The heft in the seasons.
Knowledge in the bare ankle under water
amid the rows of rice seedlings. The dialogue
of the silent back and forth, the people moving
together in flat fields of water with the patina
of the sky upon it, the green shoots rising up
from the mud, sticking up seamlessly above the water.
The water buffalo stepping through as they work,
carrying the weight of their bodies along the rows.
The wrists of the people wet under the water,
planting or pulling up. It is this Earth that all
meaning is. If love unfolds, it unfolds here.
Here where Heaven shows its face. Christ's agony
flowers into grace, spikes through the hands
holding the body in place, arms reaching wide.
It breaks our heart on Earth. Ignorance mixed
with longing, intelligence mixed with hunger.
The genius of night and sleep, being awake
and at work. The sacred in the planting, the wading
in mud. Eating what is here. Fish, bread, tea, rice.

Another Day in Paradise

It is seven o'clock this morning.
Jeni looks up and smiles. Ti is scrubbing clothes
on her knees out back. Bu Fat is hardly visible
in the unlit kitchen. Lili picks up the tray
by the open doorway. Jeni is grinding a sauce.
Ti is dumping water from a plastic bucket
with one hand, making a splashing sound on cement.
Bu Su walks as if balancing something on her head.
Jeni smiles and speaks very slowly without sound.
Lili is cutting pork fat into small squares
on the bench. Ti is on her knees washing dishes.
Bu Fat is folding wonton close up to the counter.
Bu Su is carrying a tray of dirty dishes
into the kitchen without any expression.
Jeni stirs the pork frying in the wok. Lili is
cutting vegetables. Bu Su is frying onions
and laying them out to drain. The rice is steaming.
Ti is carrying a tray of food. Bu Fat is lifting
water from the reservoir in the kitchen. Someone
is sweeping. Two are washing the floor on their knees
with their backs to me, side by side. All have taken
baths with cold water and are wearing nice clothes.
All of them waiting in the big, now-empty restaurant.
They sit together at one of the tables. *Tedour,*
I say. Jeni says *Tedour* without making any sound.
One says, *Salammat Malan* and I say the same.
It is nine o'clock. They walk out into the dark night.

Lovers in the Size of God's Hand

Mostly what you can see now is the hills.
But she is there, very small and far away,
walking by the sea, looking for blue
everlasting. He is lying by the well
dreaming of owls and stars (all of them).
The two of them are separated
but together in the distance.
She carries the dark inside herself,
he carries the light. They are married
by the difference and vastness.
They eat bread together as a practice.
Distance adds up step by step,
hour by hour, day by day into years.
The waves breaking beside her
are as loud as the voice of God,
and as strong as the stillness
by the well. One calls, *Here, here.*
The other repeating, *Yes, here.*

Heavy with Things and Flesh

Crowing. And a neighbor man already up.
Sun in the air above water.
Sunlight on a rock wall.
Sunlight on my floor.
Wind in the heat. A woman
in her farmhouse talking
to someone outside. Along with
hobbled goats in a field.
At eight in the evening
a man in his heavy wooden boat
is repairing the holes in
the yellow net piled around him.
I came here exhausted in my heart.
And will go back the same way.
The gods do sit at our table.
But when they leave, we don't follow.

A Thirst Against

There is a hunger for order,
but a thirst against. What if
every time a flower forms in the mind,
something gives it away to time?
Leaf by petal, by leaf. As if the soul
were a blotter of this world—
of the greater, the wetter, the more
tired, the more torn. All singing,
but no song. Hamlet darker than night.
And poor Ophelia less than the flowers
she wore. Both lost. One dead,
the other to follow soon.
One too heavy, one too frail.
Both finding themselves among the fallen.
Each time I think, it is here
that God lives. Right around here,
in this terrible, ruined place
with streets made desolate by neon,
in midwinter and freezing winds.
In these Chicago avenues.

The Limits of Desire

Love came along and said, "I know,
I know. Abandoned after all
those promises.
But I can't help. I traffic
in desire, passion, and lust.
Trade bread for more bread,
change blood into wine.
I take the heaviest things
and make them joyous."
We sit under the fig tree.
How fragrant she is, her hand
over the folds of her dress.
Head bowed, voice quiet
in the warm wind.

Always Mistaken

We see the ocean and hear
its noise as two different things.
We know they should be experienced
at the same time, but no one understands
how to do it. We can't decide whether
to be instructed by the white birds
flying ("Going to the source,"
as someone says), or to see them
as another aimless beauty
to be remembered with pleasure.
Everybody has a subject and they
take turns: peaches, new clothes,
lying naked alone on the porch
with the sun. Horses in shade
under bay trees by the creek.
Sex and kissing at the same time.
We never understood the life
we lived, nor the one now.
There is a clue. On Earth, the dance.
In Heaven, a table set with bowls
of rice and cups of tea.

They Tell Me It's Over

I say, "I stayed in Motel 6, where you told me
to stay." He says, "I meant The Chicago Inn."
That was this winter's visit. That was a year.

The Passion

What is death to the man who is already dead?
What are cucumbers to him, or the color
of the sea? Surely the people God loves most,
and trusts more, are passionate.
They listen to the wind in dry wild grass.
They know what is beautiful survives
in those who contain the farthest place.
It is true that the voice of heaven promises
a place without hunger or thirst. But clearly
it is not harmony, peace, or wisdom we see
in the face of the risen Christ. It is
the carnage of rapture, lovers transformed
into glory by the crucifixion of their hearts.

Arkansas Afternoons

Today I took the postmaster's advice and found
Nina May, "who will talk to anyone," he said.
I needed to find how to get my quilt-tops backed.
Following his map, I drove behind Goshen
to the small square and the dots
that meant pine trees. There she was
in her house that looked out on fields.
She draped the four tops over a card table
and named each design: bow tie, snail,
nines. Then told me the story of how
she almost died a week ago.
She showed me a big pot of turnips she was
cooking, gave me the recipe. Gave me a glass
of Dr Pepper. Answered the phone
and told a sick friend she would call back
if her mind held out. She never answered
any of my questions about the quilts.
Said she would take care of them after
she got well, that we could go to see her
friend Pearl, did I want her to mend
the old tops. Went on about the blue
and yellow. "One might look good with
an edge that had a small design to balance
the top's boldness," she said.
I was saying inside, "Good-bye, good-bye,
my love. The great love of my life."
Waving like an Italian woman,
shamelessly. Knowing everything was lost
four years ago. Waving to no one now.

Hard Season

Already this spring the lilacs are failing,
in pieces and chunks, the way rust
ruins metal everywhere.
It doesn't take much of that before
she begins not to care. Which makes her
want to rip the flawed flowers
maliciously from the bushes, seeing how
wind and butterflies and blossoming
can be confused with feeling.
Love lives on the mountain with calm
and counterweight. In the center,
with the presence, in the sunlight.

How It Works

I will tell you a story about
how death works. One year
when he was hunting,
my father lay down
by a cliff on the top
of a mountain.
As he lay there mostly asleep,
he heard a breathing
close to his face.
The breathing of a mountain
lion. When he looked,
there was no lion.
When he rolled over
and looked down the ledge
he saw a great eagle
an arm-reach away
hovering over a huge space.

Io: Shape-Shifted

You heard it from a distance.
Saw me turning into a cow
and tortured by your wife's bees.
Imagine my hand turning
into a hoof, tender flesh becoming
soft calfhide. Nose to snout,
breasts shoved between flanks,
stomach reshaping itself.
Eyes enlarging and moving
to the sides of my head. Then plunging
into the sea, mooing with fear,
salt water in my mouth and the darkness
below me. Beginning inside.
So vast an event, so much becoming.

God-Singing

A voice rises from the mosque farther down the mountain,
and slides from octave to octave, drifting into this orchard,
mixing with the song of a youth's yearning. The workers
let each know it is their turn with a quick laugh, or two
women jointly calling something back to him. All of it,
especially the laughing, feels very young, presexual.
Worker songs, beyond speech but never far from feeling.
Before marriage, before adult life, and after.
Both voices hover after amid the white blossoming.
The trees do not need or benefit from either, but brighten
whenever the sun is laid bare of the mist. The apple trees
are like women in formal dresses standing in the giant
courtrooms of this oriental kingdom of Heaven, not waiting
or still. Their only mission is in the abundance
of their being, their standing. The same as the bird
that sings now, sharp and quick. All of this in unison,
neither young nor old, neither bird nor human.

"Why does this city still retain / its ancient
rights over my thoughts and feelings?"

I did not tell you because I thought
it was a story, and I don't tell stories.
And because it isn't quite a story.
Mischa was there on the couch
next to Joseph. When he crossed
the living room, I touched the soft leather
of his shoe. But that's not the story.
I did not think of it until now.
They sat together, two expatriates
talking in Russian about how to design
his *Nutcracker.* Mischa would get up
and dance a passage or two, then sit down
and talk some more. They already knew
life was tragic. That was their weight.
Yet it was different with them.
They knew and were still capable. Even now
when Joseph is dead and Mischa's not
dancing much. But what I wanted
to tell you about was not that.
What I wanted to tell you was after
that when they were talking Russian again.

Everyday Rice

Some kinds of love
leave only wreckage behind, as war does.
The world creates itself out of the debris.
Greece at its finest left ruins
and the clanging silence. The world keeps
the damage along with the patches of light
between these overlapping branches of aspen.
Akhmatova used Dostoyevsky's description
of Kirilov after he hanged himself,
dangling near the cupboard.
There is the smell of narcissus blooming
as I walk across the cabin to rinse the rice
five or six times before making it into dinner.

Stuff

High up there she saw what
survives in the violent sunlight.
And felt no particular emotion.
The sea below, stone.

        Circle that.

The wind in the bright heat
made a sound like winter.
The wind moving strongly
in the whitening wild wheat.

        Circle *whitening*.

Goat, poppies, dry creek bed.

        Circle all of it.

Parts of sentences: *bleached
in the thin far-away,
momentary, and.*
A veil in her mind moved,
momentarily uncovering
memory and *of.* She felt
dazed by *facts* and *cared-for.*

        Circle *facts*.

The Unknowing

I lie in the palm of its hand. I wake in the quiet,
separate from the air that's moving the trees outside.
I walk on its path, fall asleep in its darkness.
Loud sounds produce this silence. One of the markers
of the unknown, a thing in itself. To say
When I was in love gives birth to something else.
I walk on its path. The food I put in my mouth.
The girl I was riding her horse is not a memory
of desire. It is the place where the unknown
was hovering. The shadow in the cleavage
where two mountains met. The dark trees
and the shade and moving shadows there
where the top of the mountain stops and meets
the light much bigger than it is.
Its weight against all the light. A birthplace
of the unknown, the quick, the invisible.
I would get off my horse and lie down there,
let the wind from the ocean blow the high grass over
my body, be hidden with it, be one of its secrets.

Trying to Tack

"You are the great love of my life," he said.
"I will stop eating until you agree."
Then he pushed a safety pin into the skin
over his heart. Fastened it there.
His sister took a picture of his chest
which he took to the woman
along with his love poem
that had a Cyclone fence in it
and a city, and wind.
Six years later she lives alone
with quiet and nature.
She has not forgotten anything.
She drives the ghosts away like Ulysses
at the gate of Hell beating the spirits back,
waiting for Tiresias who can tell
how to sail home against the wind.

Fiefdom

In the tea garden of the Muslim graveyard
(three small tables with chairs) the clamor
of Istanbul is dulled by the trees
and simplicity, and the stillness
of the dead people below. An old man comes
to take the order for the only thing he sells.
Returns with two glasses of bitter tea,
two cubes of sugar and a small tin spoon
on each saucer. The quiet is in the idea
of silence. Like the heavy iron fence
all around, and the cat who runs away
into her world of stone paths, tombs,
dirt, bushes, and her small sounds.

George Oppen

It had been a fine day.
We walked on Mount Tamalpais,
white sailboats on the blue bay
and the Pacific Ocean behind the three of us.
Ordinary days in the difficult years
when his intricate mind was draining away.
The afternoon I spilled red wine on the white
tablecloth while Mary was frying hamburgers.
I wanted to cry. It confused him and he said
would I like to live there. When I went
to the window, he put his hand on me.
His mind had gone astray. His books
in the living room, read so often some were
held together by rubber bands. There were
wadded-up poems behind an open door.
There was pity and crying out as the dark
overwhelmed him, driving him down.

Meanwhile

Strange short trees, views of the mountain.
One overlapping the other. Rain while I swam
in the heated pool of someone's hotel.
Fish with slivered ginger, fresh bamboo,
et cetera. The men came to see me
at the restaurant where I lived. Arabian,
Chinese, Javanese. Bringing food and music,
flowers and invitations. Stories that always
had to do with power and hints
of the darkness in sex. Me caring so little.
Grateful for their desire, but indifferent.

The Universe on Its Own

Nature without shape, the universe without form.
Rubble, mistakes, lies, things thrown away.
Shapes we can only guess at. Leveled, broken,
strewn, lost. Maybe the picture on a shard
of a young goat hanging from somebody's shoulder.
Maybe only a black triangle with white splotches
overlapping like swarms in the sky at night,
like bees looking for a new home. The shape of love
is a scattering. The meaning we resist. The world
as far as we can see random in a wind.

In the Half-Light

Naked women playing happily behind
the bamboo wall. Washing their hair,
talking as they carry babies about
in the white steam from the pool.
Wet young boys with small penises
jump noisily on top of each other.
A woman stands alone in a purple top
wrapping the skirt snugly around,
then wrapping a belt around and around
from hipbone to breasts. She puts on
a blouse and crosses the clearing.
Goes up the steps into the hills.
Dragonfly and water lily. A bird
in the air flutters its wings just after
the rain stops. Then it is dark. Love
gone from me for three years now.

Downsized

She lives where no one comes to visit.
In an old house made of stone and wood,
with bamboo ceilings. When she goes down
to the village, she says good evening
in a foreign language to the old people
sitting outside on the streets of rock.
They are the only words she speaks all day.
This morning when she opened
his letter to read again, a scorpion
fell out on her white cotton nightgown.
"Each day," she thinks later, "I am less
and less part of the world, even though
I live closer to it than ever."

It Was Important

to outstrip death with theater.
Something unnatural to dazzle the brain,
Never the reality of Bill giving me
the 17th century pavans from *Lachrimae*
before shooting himself in the stomach.
Or George Oppen's stubborn clarity
turned into fear at the end,
passing beyond what he could endure.
We are slaughtered either way,
and the gods don't care.

Paul on the Road to Damascus

The soul is an emblem so bright
you close your eyes. As when the sun
here comes up out of the sea and blazes
on the white of a village called Lefkes.
The soul is dark in its nature, but shines.
A rooster crows. The tall grass
stirs on the ruined ancient terraces.
The shadow of a wafting crocheted curtain
runs in a slant down the wall of a house,
as the Albanians paving the street below
are banging pieces of marble
against a metal wheelbarrow.

The Old Songs

I

The birds far away in the air
come only just before the rain.

II

I hear the nothingness with eyes open.
My heart fills with it
like a peach I ate all of.
I dream of the next country of me.
A land of shining rivers, the two silences
and the wind. Arriving there, ashes
smudged on my forehead. Until August
the fifteenth when Mary rises
in bridal satin, her body rinsed
by the white silence.

III

I need as the rose needs
water and good earth.
It repeats itself again and again.
The wetness here is my pleasure.
The excess of chilies
in the noodles pleases me.
No matter what, the painted birds
flutter among the trees.
I discovered the garbage
in the alleys of the bright
village smells sweet.

I am gradually understanding
the life of the birds in the sky.

IV

Christ with His silverness
is not visible now.
Belief has leaked out
of the hearts of men.
I learned this from the man
who tied love up with a rope
and beat it to death with
a board. These monuments
are black with age. Voices call
out to God from their loud-
speakers all night, each night,
and no voice answers.

V

I sing the small songs of the soul,
because the soul sees itself like that.
I see the soul the way the morning
light sees the Parthenon,
as Oedipus saw Colonus. The soul
moving the dark around.

Old Pictures in a New Land

Dirt Bird Hedge Light Scent. A commonwealth.
Angels and imitations of God in every church.
Everyone was helpless when it came to leaves.
The bower where the lovers and would-be
lovers wandered boldly and decorously
devouring each other in each other's
dilated pupils. The lady in a lavish gown
amid the leaves. Her hands crossed over
each other over her belly. A little music
in the air, night-faint. And exactly few words.
Far between (rain matters). Something here
knows a dwelling place. A primitive home.
Who took corn? The old glass in the windows
made the world waver. The door looked like
a fort with fire inside. Echo. Loneliness.
Fear. An ur-book, a picture of another place.
A woman in a stiff dress. Leaves just like
the leaves on the new trees all around
there in the world called new or far away.
And a color. Pewter. Blue. Any color but green.

Like Lot's Wife

The Italian town is empty.
It was built well
but nobody moved in.
She is there maybe
looking for someone.
She won't find him.
She stands in the middle
of the day, blasted
by brightness. In silence.
The stillness meeting
the stillness inside her.

A Mountain Facing a Mountain

What poetry demands is worse
than nakedness, and less knowable.
A woman with dark hair, maybe,
at the front door of her house
on a mountain, the earth
sloping down in the dusty
olive trees.
When there are no crops,
the winnowing ring fills
with weeds. The wind blows
through history, not dancing,
leaving no harvest, keeping
its virtue, its own separateness.

Music at a Distance

Only twice has anyone
asked me to sing.
Once was the man I loved
in a run-down section of Chicago.
I sang my father's favorite,
"Shenandoah." *Away, you rolling
river.* Now it's seven years later,
and I am living on an island.
There is only my stillness
and the absence.
And the sound of me singing.

Backstage

Oma is the oldest woman in the house.
She tells me stories. Remembers everything.
All the dresses for her wedding,
the ruined house with the precious bird nests.
What it was like when she was little,
and what happened to her husband's diamonds.
But when I wanted to know about
when the Japanese came, she looked down,
saying she didn't remember.
On the Day of the Dead, Oma worked for hours
cooking the special foods. Finally came
and took me by the hand. Led me
to a part of the house I had never seen.
To an empty room with an altar, incense,
and a long table. A place set for each
ancestor with rice and homemade sausage.
Baked stew with a potato on top.
She insisted I sit at the table.
A different Oma stood proudly watching
me struggle to swallow the food for the dead.
The powerful geese outside filled the silence,
squawking like offended clergy.

The Part Left Over

It's as though I were an event
on this mountain, not merely the evidence.
Plainness and heat.
Bleached grass all the way
to the fig tree and the sea silent
far below. Sound of a lizard
disappearing into darkness
between rocks. Memories and the dream.
Insects, thorns, no shade, shards.
The face of a man on a broken vase
listening to someone on a missing fragment.
No language for the part of me
left over. A clay piece of just the hand
of a woman, two fingers touching
the front of her draped garment.
The special beauty of what's absent.

Hephaestus Alone

His heart is like a boat that sets forth alone
on the ocean and goes far out from him,
as Aphrodite proceeds on her pleasure journeys.
He pours the gold down the runnels
into a great mystery under the sand.
When he pulls it up by the feet
and knocks off the scale, it is a god.
What is it she finds with those men
that equals this dark birthing? He makes
each immortal manifest. The deities
remain invisible in their pretty gardens
of grass and violets, of daffodils and jasmine.
Even his wife lives like that. Going on yachts,
speaking to the captains in the familiar.
Let them have it, the noons and rain and joy.
He makes a world here out of frog songs
and packed earth. He made his wife
so she contains the green-fleshed
melons of Lindos, thalo blue of the sea,
and one ripe peach at five in the morning.
He fashioned her by the rules, with love,
made her with rage and disillusion.

The Right People

I liked everything about the gods.
Strong naked men in the clearest light,
women with their breasts showing.
And the way their thin gowns
draped, the layering and flow.
Interested in passion rather than exceeding.
Willing to understand nothing about love.
Which is why I am looking
at the flowering caper bush
that contains what I know about the Earth
creating the eternal out of itself
without rising above or letting go.

Waking Up Happy

Love didn't work, doesn't work,
hasn't worked in four thousand years.
We listen to the rain.
We listen to the quiet.
To a universe beyond anything
we are made of.
Love dead all night
for these seven years in a row.
I wake up alone in the cool morning
light, before the sun is visible.

The Secrets of Poetry

Very long ago when the exquisite celadon bowl
that was the mikado's favorite cup got broken,
no one in Japan had the skill and courage
to mend it. So the pieces were taken back
to China with a plea to the emperor
that it be repaired. When the bowl returned,
it was held together with heavy iron staples.
The letter with it said they could not make it
more perfect. Which turned out to be true.

The Tree Falling in a Vacant Forest

The window open. Hearing
the summer wind in the dark trees.
Offering up silence
to the given silence.
Farther up the mountain
are stone paths between
walls of piled-up rocks
protecting abandoned fields.
The church bells ring once
at one and nobody stirs.
Mute, alive and awake.
Stillness so much like prayer,
so much like death.
The dreadful distance
between one person
and another. Each one
listening to that single high note
in all the singing.
Each one hearing the same one.

Deeper in the Jungle, the River Divides

Death rewrites the script, and love does not.
Love is remembered by its memory
and its truth. Death keeps things in a zigzag
way, claims for itself what it does not deserve.
We live with the black and white, and in
the color of it. All of it. The bay tree.
A moment of Sophocles. The man who loved me.
And the self. The fragments remembering wholeness.
A dream of a Go set on the table in my room
where a friend comes every day, moving a stone
each time. A game lasting year after year.

Harmonica

Gone like the fish in water
The rock on the road
A dove on the sill of the soul

Love is gone like a rock in water
A dove in the air
Sun that was on the mountain

Fish up the stream
Buckeyes flowering
Horse on the hill

House on the other side
of the hill

At Risk

This body does not smell human,
it smells of oregano in heat.
This is not your world
where people work and live in a house.
It is a place before or after.
After and before that.
Things in parts and pieces.
The wind turning silver
in the olive trees.
A red pomegranate on the table.
Silence with a ringing in it.
This is a beginning
or long afterwards.
Exactly that.

Lost in the Heart

The crazy woman at the beginning of the mountain
spends her days on the dirt road,
her face painted white. A man walks by
with his arms raised, holding empty
cigarette packages, the back of his pants ripped
and his underpants torn, showing the brown skin
of his bottom. Safety is not the answer.
Nor loving kindness. So I leave
Kuan Yin's temple to protect the loneliness
of each one there. The soiled moon is one
day too old. What was easy to pity
is no longer fine. The world is stronger
than ideas about the world. I walk home
knowing the moon rides the night as strongly
as ever. But my heart does not look up.

Ariadne Writes to Theseus at Random

You have been away so long
I have stopped asking visitors
if they have seen or heard of you.
For years I tried to learn the best
to show you when you came back.
What hour and what path for going
to the beach. What week to gather
oregano and in which field.
But the world is just what it is.
A plate of olives that are olives.
Fresh bread that is bread.
The world of this island
where you left me. The sound
of the sea's constant breathing.
All of it together the music
around the silence in my heart.

Paying the Price

The man who lived in sweet illusions
is dying. He lived in a dream of women,
and he is dying. He is an old man now,
living in a world of ruined loves.
With his frail wife who talks endlessly.
In a house in the dangerous part of town.
He has just been told he has cancer.
All of a sudden he needs money.
His car doesn't work. He is wrecked
in the worn-out world of believing.
His wife has been ill for years.
He eats the lima beans with frozen peas
she cooks every night. He is wrecked,
naked, dying. And he survives.
Stubbornly, with empty longing. Doting
on the fine roses in his weedy backyard.

17399 Edgewood Road, Fayetteville, Arkansas

A few days before I am to move
out of this house (where you have
never been) I find myself
standing in this empty room
watching the quilt
hanging on the clothesline,
remembering the black-and-white
cows out back. Remembering how
the soft air would come in the half-open
kitchen window. The beauty
of the glass all clean
and the light shining through.

Finding the Way

FOR JUDITH BROWN

Today I went to the village church
where bells rang steadily
for a special ceremony.
Outside were baskets full of bread
as the body of Christ. I discovered
the Greeks believe God's body has
the flavor of sesame and cumin.

Stubborn

I take the alley instead of the street,
reach up to see if I can reach
the lowest rung of the fire escape.
I have a ladder instead of a church,
dreams of boats and memories of ships.
I have eyes for the future and eyes
for escape, to leave love alone.
The song of heavenly romance flies
over the dark fields and into the woods
where I have come. I hear the music
but can see nothing, carrying the grief.
Giving it to no one.

The Muchness

She went back,
knowing the way in her marrow.
Trees in leaf but joyless, ceremonial.
Lit with the Underworld's slum light.
A small, ordinary apartment.
Iron heater, remnants
of the heart's quiet,
of the mind's radiance.
A wooden chair and three windows.
Wobbly table in the kitchen,
lily plant on the linoleum.
In the darkest room the bed.
And the trunk open.
She opens the window an inch.
All around her a world that used to be.

Wrapping Stones

Everything I am is what survived
love's leaving. Everything I see, eat, want,
have is what survived the goneness
of what love is. Love, like time, takes down
the house, leaving only the partial walls,
open squares of light for windows,
and a door. The people here wrap
their special stones in large tea leaves.
I walked back from that looking for
a fallen bamboo the right length
for drying kimonos, thinking what
a surprise it is that even such a love
becomes familiar like everything else.
I kept a place for it, stubborn, blessed.
Even through the six years of pain after.
Now it's like the sun going down
each day. Or the moon changing size
predictably all along its range of feeling.
Dies and comes again. But love is
like the salmon that have not come back
to Walker Creek for the last three years.

A Kind of Victory

God moves as the moon in its arc moves.
He marries us beyond all government.
Brings us to a meadow where four deer
are dying, arrows in their wounds.
In the distance we can hear trampling
and shouts. There was a sacredness
we carried. As sure as a bird flying with a twig
in its beak. When the soldiers arrive
and demand that we come out of the bushes,
we walk out sadly, and surrender.

Winning

There is having by having
and having by remembering.
All of it a glory, but what is past
is the treasure. What remains.
What is worn is what has lived.
Death is too familiar, even though
it adds weight. Passion adds size
but allows too much harm.
There is a poetry that asks for
this life of silence in midday.
A branch of geranium in a glass
that might root. Poems of time
now and time then, each
containing the other carefully.

Acknowledgments

Grateful acknowledgment is made to the editors of the following journals in which these poems first appeared:

The American Poetry Review: "The Secrets of Poetry," "Etiology," "More than New," "The Spirit Neither Sorts nor Separates," "As Being Is Eternal," "Io: Shape-Shifted," "Hard Season," "A Thirst Against," "Gypsy Kings"

The Bellingham Review: "Always Mistaken," "A Mountain Facing a Mountain"

Boston Review: "Calamities: Another Eden"

Columbia: A Journal of Literature and Art: "God-Singing," "Alone with the Goddess," "The Old Songs"

Crab Orchard Review: "The Muchness," "So Different from Heaven," "Arkansas Afternoons," "Winning," "Harmonica," "Not a Pretty Bird," "The Heart Flowing Out"

Five Fingers Review: "The Center of Intent," "George Oppen"

Green Mountains Review: "In the Half-Light," "The Right People," "The Passion," "The Unknowing," "Paul on the Road to Damascus," "The Empty Bowl," "A Kind of Victory," "The Universe on Its Own"

Harvard Review: "Fiefdom," "Finding the Way," " 'Why does this city still retain / its ancient rights over my thoughts and feelings?' "

N.Y. Arts Magazine: "Another Day in Paradise"

TriQuarterly: "Hephaestus Alone," "The Calves Not Chosen," "Fish Tea Rice," "The Precision"

I want to thank the Lannan Foundation for giving me a completion grant that helped me to finish this book. I also want to thank the Robert Francis Trust for allowing me to live in his house for a year in which some of this poetry was written.

LINDA GREGG is the author of *Chosen by the Lion, The Sacraments of Desire, Alma,* and *Too Bright to See.* Her work has appeared in *The New Yorker,* the *Paris Review,* the *Kenyon Review,* and the *Atlantic Monthly,* among other literary journals, magazines, and anthologies. Gregg grew up in Marin County, California, has traveled extensively, and has taught writing at numerous conferences, colleges, and universities.

This book was designed by Wendy Holdman. It is set in Charlotte Book by Stanton Publication Services, Inc., and manufactured by Bang Printing on acid-free paper.

Graywolf Press is dedicated to the creation and promotion of thoughtful and imaginative contemporary literature essential to a vital and diverse culture. For further information, visit us online at: *www.graywolfpress.org*.